Winter in the Woods

Written by Linda Ruggieri
Illustrated by Carolyn Ewing

WR Weekly Reader Corporation
Inspire the future.™

Please visit our Web site at www.weeklyreader.com
For a free color catalog describing Weekly Reader Books, call 1-800-446-3355

Weekly Reader Books fax: 1-856-786-3360

Library of Congress Cataloging-in-Publication Data

Ruggieri, Linda
Winter in the Woods by Linda Ruggieri
Illustrated by Carolyn Ewing

Art direction and page layout: Tammy Gruenewald and Michele McLean
Contributing editor: Sue LaBella

Summary: A poem about animals in the woods and the
tracks the animals make in the snow

Includes bibliographical reference and index.

ISBN 0–8374-0006-6 (library binding)
ISBN 0–8374-0007-4 (softcover)

1. Seasons—Juvenile literature.   2. Animals—Juvenile literature
(1. Seasons. 2. Animals.   3.Snow)   I. Title.

This edition first published in 2003 by
Weekly Reader
200 First Stamford Place
PO Box 120023
Stamford, CT   06912-0023 USA
Copyright © 2003 by Weekly Reader Books

Printed in Brazil

Note to Educators and Parents:

Reading opens up a whole new world of knowledge, adventure, and excitement for children, yet we know that teaching a child to read can be challenging. Studies show that every child learns differently, so providing a variety of reading materials is important.

Weekly Reader, a premier leader in educational publishing, has developed a new picture-book collection called Weekly Reader Little Books, a series of Weekly Reader Books. Created by Weekly Reader editors, the collection is aimed at children aged 3 to 6 who are just learning to read. We have designed the books for teachers to use in the classroom or for parents to use at home.

Each themed set contains four books that are engaging, topical, and based on material covered in other Weekly Reader materials. The child-sized books feature colorful illustrations and simple text. Each book includes a glossary and activities that invite children to become active learners.

In the themed set Seasons, children will learn about various characteristics of each season.

Weekly Reader Little Books help teach children many important basic reading skills, including these:

• holding a book and turning pages • reading for information
• identifying words using pictures as clues • reading from left to right and from top to bottom • recognizing letter sounds (phonological awareness)
• reading words and sentences accurately and smoothly (fluency)

We hope you will introduce your beginning readers to the Weekly Reader Little Books and to the wonderful world of reading!
—Weekly Reader Editors

Words You Will Learn

cardinal: a bright red American songbird

porcupine: an animal covered with hair and long, sharp spikes called quills

tracks: marks made when something has passed by

waddling: walking from side to side with short steps

An animal made tracks in the snow.
Can you name the animal?

A rabbit made the tracks.
It was hopping in the snow.

**An animal made tracks in the snow.
Can you name the animal?**

**A porcupine made the tracks.
It was waddling in the snow.**

An animal made tracks in the snow.
Can you name the animal?

A deer made the tracks.
It was walking in the snow.

**Many animals made tracks in the snow.
Can you name the animals?**

Whose Tracks Are These?

Look at the tracks in the snow. Move your finger
from the animal to the tracks it made.

Try This! Look carefully. How many times
can you find the cardinal in the book?